Golden Motes

Conrad and Gail,
Wishing you many
golden motes moments.
            Carol

Golden Motes

**A
collection of writing
by the faculty of
the College of Education
Eastern Oregon University**

Edited by

Carol Lauritzen

All proceeds from the sale of *Golden Motes* will benefit the Education Student Crisis Scholarship Fund of the Eastern Oregon University Foundation.

All inquiries should be directed to:
College of Education
Eastern Oregon University
One University Blvd.
La Grande, OR 97850

Cover Art: Jan Dinsmore

Editor's Note

The inspiration for this book came from two streams. The first was a desire to provide financial support to students in their final months of becoming a teacher. Each faculty member in a teacher preparation program has the privilege of becoming acquainted with outstanding teacher candidates. Many of these future teachers have made amazing personal sacrifices to obtain their educations. One young woman was subsisting on ramen noodles during most of her student teaching term. Another sold her wedding china and crystal to pay for tuition. A single mother told me that if she could just afford four more hours of baby-sitting a week, she could be more successful as a student teacher. Other students have gone into debt to be able to pay for the exams required for licensure. Stories like these were the motivation for creating the Education Student Crisis Scholarship Fund in the Eastern Oregon University Foundation. Students may apply to the fund for financial support in times of need. But the fund needed to grow in order to support as many students as possible. The usual fundraisers were considered. Unlike the music department, we couldn't "put on a show" and unlike the athletic department, we couldn't put on a sports event. Just as I was pondering the possibilities, a poem appeared in my email from Kerri Wenger. It made me realize that my colleagues were a talented group of writers and with their contributions we could create a book. *Golden Motes* is the result of this effort.

My thanks go to each faculty member who contributed a piece of writing, a photograph or the cover design. Rick Mack provided enthusiasm for the project as well as publishing "how-to." Nancy Attebury of Mt. Emily Press graciously contributed the ISBN and led me through the process of obtaining a barcode. Megan, Debby, Janet and Beth answered all sorts of questions and are a terrific support staff.

This book is dedicated to all the teacher education students who will receive scholarships funded by its sale. May you become great teachers!

Carol Lauritzen
June 1, 2011

Contents

Hurrahing in Harvest—eastern Oregon style
Kerri Jo Wenger

One sundown ago
I drove our rural road alone
behind a wooden-sided onion truck.
A gentle float of flaky skins
(from pearly orbs
mounded up like ornaments)
trailed offside along our dusty way.

As we drove, that wooden truck and I,
a football wind rushed us hard.
In a sudden instant we were tackled,
showered in a gold confetti squall.

Struck, I stopped among those gilded
     wrappings
dancing in the last of evening's light.
A swirling cloud of light-filled skins.
A spinning paper constellation
thrown for yards against the gold-lined field
     of autumn sky.

It was very fine:
the road
the golden motes
and I.

Kauai #1

Heather Stanhope

Poems Are
Kerri Jo Wenger

Poems are
language
in
concentrate.

frozen O.J.,
lemonade,
lime-ade words --
distilled
and
sharp.

Dig a spoon in:

crystal-ice ideas
clink cold on teeth
and
quick-shrink
cheeks

Poems are
language
in
concentrate.

Between father and me
Michael Jaeger

Between father and me, two things,
"Laurel and Hardy" and "Victory at Sea."
The old Crosley barely receiving
Snowy monochrome images
Through constant attention
To vacuum tubes and antenna direction.

Saturdays,
Stanley carries that endless board,
His thin face and drooping chin
Crumbling into his signature weep.
Oliver flipping his tie,
Getting clunked on the head
Those pudgy cheeks
Incredulous, exasperated,
"Here's another nice mess…"
We howled at the slapstick.

Sundays, the cruisers, destroyers,
        landing craft
Hit the beaches of the South Pacific.
Tarawa, Guadalcanal, Iwo Jima, Leyte.
Never much talk, save quietly, on occasion,
"That could have been my LST."
Boat cans flapped open.
Men waded through chest high water.
On the beach they ran and fell and died.

I dared a few questions,
he a few brief answers:
"Tended the boat engine."
"Landed the men."
"Secured the beach."
"Got the generators running for the radio."
Comrades cleaved inches away.
His vision more vivid than TV.

It always seemed I had two dads,
The happy go lucky guy
      who laughed out loud
At vaudeville humor
And the man returned from seven invasions
Memory of water and sand and blood.

In the Blood
Donald Wolff

Lately, I've been telling friends how my son
in the first year of his computer science
major took a philosophy course to round out
his schedule, and had to say, in his first
paper, he couldn't contradict Schopenhauer's
view that pain is a positive in life—is what
we all have in common—while pleasure is
the negative—the party we throw ourselves
when pain abates for a time, gives our due,
arbitrarily, to someone else . . . and it
reminded me of a visit home thirty-five years
ago, after my first year of graduate school,
when in order to afford a pound of ground
round once a week, I became a grader for a
professor teaching a course in continental
literature where we read *Magic Mountain*, so
that at home when I told my mother that it
had become my favorite novel, out of the

blue she declares of my father, about whom I knew nothing since he drank himself to death when I was nine months old, that it was his favorite also and here's his first edition, pulling it out of God knows where, after all that time.

Nag

Sharon Porter

Hard to imagine my dad at seventeen. To see his smile spread all across, not tightened by responsibility. Maybe his flannel shirt pulled out at the waist, from morning chores. I can imagine him slowly shaking his head the day before at the plans being served up by his cousins, Junior and Bobby, his stomach lurching like a truckgate ride over a sharp dip in the road. He might have thought 'What breeds this creativity?" It may have been the hot sun, a shimmer of heat over the tiresome expanse of rustling cornfields, or the dread of spending a day cutting jimson weed out of the soybeans. Whatever the spark, Dad's cousins had bargained with their dad for an escapade. They were getting to bury their old farm horse, Sammy.

The brothers' morning chores were frantically done. Their two old milk cows,

Elsie and Dolly, blinked at the flurry in the stalls. They were used to having their milk squirted every whichaway but the bucket. The most recent game was to try to accomplish a direct hit to the bam cat's mouth. A polite stream wasn't an objective. The shooter got more points for an eye splash or an ear bath. A short- lived game (the cat was getting smarter) Junior and Bobby turned their attention to this summer's game involving horse flies. Like city boys perfecting the flight of paper airplanes, Dad's cousins would catch a horsefly and run a length of straw up its behind. Turning it loose would produce an aerial show worthy of the Blue Angels. The variables were length of the straw, size of the horsefly, and the usual flight considerations of wind current and velocity. But that day, all of their childish diversions were set aside for the encounter with the largest dead creature they would ever bury.

   I'll bet my dad was pretty excited that morning, riding over with his father in their rusty‐ red 1940 Chevy truck. It was nothing to look at, a real beater, but it got from field to farm somewhat reliably. The backfires scared the mule from time to time. He would hightail it to the far corner of the pasture. 'Junior and Bobby represented an adventurous world, a far cry from Dad's studious own. A middle child of seven, he stood between his siblings as the sentinel of balance. He wasn't pulled by the silliness of the youngest nor darkened by the sullenness of the elders. He neither reacted to the calm or the storm of familial relations. He rooted there, deep and reaching. He was always the arbiter, the peacemaker, the Janus of the clan. So, when the first waft of adventure wended its way over to Dad's house, he begged his father to let him come along for the day. Burying a horse, imagine.

As soon as Bill stepped out of the truck, his cousins grabbed him by the neck and they lighted out for the burial grounds behind the back barn, a mile down the lane. The usual horseplay began at the bend in the lane, beyond sight of the house. They spied a stinkbug and stole her manure ball, gleefully observing her confusion. They tried to see how far each boy could pitch the shovel (only a shovel landing standing up counted.) Feeling the sun climb in the sky, the cousins sobered up and started digging.

Uncle John, his Caribbean blue eyes fixed on his boys, had reminded them at breakfast that the longer the hot sun did its job on ol' Sammy, the more ripe he would get. A farm kid doesn't need much imagery to respond to this motivation. You only have to see one swollen hog waiting for the "gut truck" to get the drift of his advice.

They started digging in the sandy soil beside the utility barn where ol' Sammy had been dragged there, hitched to the back of Uncle John's tractor. Strong and sinewy from summer haying, the boys began their job with gusto, hooping and hollering, hoping to finish in time to do some catfishing back at the farm pond. Just early morning, they raised a sweat after a few shovelfuls. Two hours later, the boys were flagging and silent.

They had a hole wide enough to accommodate the wide expanse of Sammy's broad back but depth was a concern. Using his shovel handle as a rough ruler, John, Jr. estimated they were deep enough to clear Sammy's knees if they could somehow just push Sammy in the grave on his back. Dinnertime almost upon them‐ the thought of Aunt Olive's beans and cornbread, and the promise of breaded catfish for supper, prompted Bobby to fashion a solution for the problem at hand. "If we cut off Sammy's legs at the knee we can quit digging now, cover him up and be fishing before supper." He looked eagerly to John, Jr.'s face for approval. Seeing Junior leaning heavily on the shovel handle, wiping through the grit to reveal a grin, Bobby tallied a vote for the plan. Looking over to Dad for consensus, my father was shaking his head from side to side, a million "no's" stinging his conscience like a sweat bee up a pants leg. "it won't work. They'll catch us, lick our hides for bein' lazy. They'll find out we didn't do the job right. They'll make us dig him up and do it over when he smells worse than today. May be maggoty by then. They'll know we'll be done too soon." He just moped over his shovel handle, delivering his speech, slow and even. "They'll, they'll, they'll Billy, you just can't work all the time. Dad's busy fixin' fence down that soybean field out behind the back barn. He won't know what time we started or when we finish. At dinner, we'll just say we're almost done." John, Jr. jumped in to seal the deal. "No one will know. It's just us, right? Who's gonna tell? And besides, I thought you loved to fish? Just think how cool your feet will feel dipped in sparkling pond water. Layin' back, face warm, feet cool." Dad furtively looked to every side, motioned his cousins to come closer. "Okay, then ... who's gonna do the sawin'?" Eyes cast down, breakfast acid rose up in the back of Dad's throat, like a moral thermometer. Seconds were counted by the slap of gritty palms on sun‐ reddened necks, warning off the sweat bees. Bobby broke off the standoff. "Well ... since I guess it was my idea ... I guess I'll have to do the sawin'." It took less than three minutes for John, Jr. to hightail it to the tool shed and return with a hand saw. It was Uncle John's old one, rusty with a rivet missing from the wooden handle. It caused a bit of a wobble on the draw but for this crude job, accuracy wasn't an issue.

Bobby took his sweet time, surveying the situation. He hunkered down, pulled his cap back, scratched his forehead and figured. Finally, Bobby made his selection. He put the rusty saw to Sammy's back right leg. My dad burbled, "I gotta go. Be right back" and headed for high weeds by the fencerow. He took his sweet time watering the dandelions. By the time Dad zipped and turned around, all he saw was Sammy's compact version, ready for lowering into his final resting place. Junior hooked two chains around the bottom of Sammy's stubs, throwing the ends of the chains over the grave to fasten to the back of Uncle John's old Farmall tractor.

Climbing onto the seat, leaving my dad to mind the chains from slipping off the stubs, Junior pulled the throttle into creeper gear and edged forward. Sammy started sliding toward the grave and with a dull thud landed square, stub‑ up in the hole. Bobby heaved the legs into the grave and resting a boot on the horse's stomach leaned in to unchain him. Peering in, Dad softly wondered, "Shouldn't we say somethin' over him?" Catching each other's eye, the brothers together intoned an emphatic "Naw!" They all grabbed their shovels and, with only their grunts and the ping of glancing rocks to punctuate the stillness, they buried Sammy.

Dragging their shovels behind them, they headed for the horse tank, fed by a windmill standing as solitary sentry to the morning's events. Cupping their hands and scooping beneath the surface of the water, the boys trickled the water through their fingers over their scorched necks. Junior flicked a few drops over to where Bobby was filling his cap and Bobby, with a practiced sling, flung a capful over at Junior. In a fury of churning water, both brothers became sopping messes oblivious to my dad hanging to his end of the tank, clear of the barrage. Arms over shoulders, the cousins headed for Aunt Olive's cornbread and beans.

They stomped to their places at the table, laid out with Aunt Olive's red- checked oilcloth. For her company she had cut some white and salmon- colored asters for the Mason jar in the center of the table. My dad's father, Elliot, was quietly discussing the straw yield on his own farm with Uncle John and looked up sharply at being interrupted. Dad sat down across from his cousins, relieved to have a reason not to talk. He set about filling his plate after the "amen" of Aunt Olive's grace. During their stories and tall tales, Bobby and Junior would glance at Dad to gauge his allegiance. They assessed him steady. Just as Aunt Olive served the rhubarb pie, my grandfather pinned Dad with "Billy, you shur are quiet. Maybe you got the fantods." Bobby offered, "Well, maybe, something's naggin' him" and jabbed Junior in the ribs as his prompt to whinny and flubber his lips like a race horse at a dead stop. "I don't reckon, Pop. Must be the heat." and Dad slumped over his rhubarb pie, twisting his fork along the plate's rim.

Dad caught two catfish that afternoon but didn't take them home that night, leaving them on the Dickerson's stringer. The ride home with his father was mercifully quiet, Elliot not being a loquacious fellow. Dad kicked at the chicken crossing his path up the driveway to the barn. It cackled a protest and lighted a few feet away, grousing and pecking at the dust. The next few days passed, with Dad conducting the same old family arbitrations, finishing the daily chores, and forking hay into the hayloft in the front barn.

On Tuesday, the next week, a rainstorm blew up and set down for two days. It was the kind of gullywasher that the Midwest is famous for. Red‐ brown rivulets etched the dusty roads into ruts. Earth's hollows turned to ponds--it was a ducks' holiday. When the rain clouds broke free to travel over West Virginia, the sun got busy and turned the landscape to a sodden sauna. That evening, at supper, my grandpa brought news from Uncle John's place. "It was the darnest thing! Seems as though ol' Sammy has done been resurrected!" At the word "Sammy," my dad straightened bolt upright at the table, wondering if anyone present could see his heart thumping. He dared to look up as his dad continued, "I guess Sammy's undertakers took a short cut and now the grave washed out things a bit. They's got four perfect posts sticking out of the mud. Could be the makings of a picnic table. Whadda you think, Billy?" Eternity passed while Dad gathered up his wits to explain. Raising his head he observed the twinkling in his father's eyes. Dad huffed out his held breath.

It wasn't until the weekend that all three cousins found themselves at the scene of their latest transgression. Standing silently at the spectacle of four perfectly- planted horse's legs rising from the earth, moments passed. Bobby offered, "I'll go get the saw."

Family

Carol Lauritzen

1873, '74, '77, '78, '81, '84, and '89.
Robert and William died in infancy of
starvation.
They were buried in unmarked graves
on a plot that became a hog pen.
Angeloah was named for his grandfather,
a hell-fire and brimstone evangelist.
What he did for a living was never known.
Clara Delilah carried her beautiful,
scandalous Italian grandmother's
      middle name
but she was none for scandal.
Henry so alienated himself
from family and neighbors
that he lived alone in a board shack
that caught fire one evening
and burned to the ground as he lay in bed.
Harry was alternately a genius
and an eccentric
who could keep an old truck running,
husbanded bees and goats,
and three mail order brides.

Jno. D. pedaled his bicycle over sand trails
to high school,
graduated from college
and returned to the home place
to make something of himself.
They all had finicky stomachs.

To Martha,
aged two and three-quarters
(with apologies to Eloise Greenfield)
Kerri Jo Wenger

Honey, I love
your eyes
your big brown eyes
beautiful round brown eyes

And when your smilin' cheeks
push your eyes into an almond shape
Honey, *every* body's face
wanna wear that *melt*in' grin!

All my family's eyes have all-ways been
blue
or grey
or cat-purr green

And my own just can't seem
to choose
a grey
or green
or blue

Your daddy's eyes are handsome
hazel-brown
one chunk
that's green
But he claims he's *never* seen
two eyes that grin as much as your eyes do

And honey, he loves
your eyes
your big brown eyes
beautiful round brown eyes

Just as much as *I* do!

David
Karyn Gomez

He haunts me with his words
    —unholy tintinnabulations in my head
At peace with God, he said,
    but not at peace with the church
Damn the church
Damn those self-righteous, holier-than-thou,
hypocritical bastards
    who called themselves Christians
Those on-fire-for-the-Lord youth
    who planned to save the world,
but apparently not David

He used to fit
A bona fide on-fire-for-the-Lord kid himself
Even had a J.O.Y. stamp—
Jesus, Others, Yourself: JOY!
    —a priority list he inked everywhere
Witnessing to the potheads on the dock
    during the youth retreat
Dark eyes shining, holding my hand,
    running to share the Good News
So confident in his naïve faith
So naïve in his confidence

The JOY left when his truth came out

A midnight phone call to my house
"I have no place to go"
He was 16
Rejected at home, unwelcome in the church,
Condemned by the youth
      who taught him J.O.Y.
It was the church that murdered him
        —not the AIDS that claimed his life
Banished to Seattle's gay subculture
A place to be
      drugged and exploited
For a confused, throwaway teen
      desperate to be valued,
A place to be
      accepted
His small walk up apartment shared
      with anonymous others
Drug paraphernalia strewn everywhere
      —daring me to stare, to judge,
      to condemn
I ignore the drunk man
      who just came out of the closet
(Coming out of the closet: funny)
Just a roommate... Leaving,
      taking his track marks with him

Small and dark, no longer handsome
      in his deathbed
Pocked, bloated, drugged—legally this time

Morphine pump pinging with each push
      of the button
He whispered a pseudo-warning
      to my husband-to-be
"You better take care of her. I'll be watching."

He met my newborn two years later
      at his gravesite
I took her there, compelled
God's mysterious ways
I can't forgive—yet—
      but a new generation lives
That newborn, now a woman herself,
      active in social justice
Working to abolish the days of rejection
      for every David.
He lives on, through this girl
who does not carry her mother's anger.
Instead, she carries the hope David lost.
I trust he's watching.

On Grieving
Kerri Jo Wenger

The big surprise,
it seems to me,
is that your heart breaks fresh
in all the smallest spaces of each day:

during quiet driving
the broken yellow lines catch your breath
between one town and the next

or in the middle of a late-night stretch
as credits roll,
when the sitcom ends

or when
(yourself alone
among the Wal-Mart shoppers
tasting melon from small plastic cups)
the kindly, nodding woman says, Oh,
I think you should take two, dear,
you really look like you could use
a boost

Oregon Coast
Scott Smith

Lines Written Running
Kerri Jo Wenger

Isn't it good what a body can do

Rock a baby
Fight flu

Listen, hard
Inhale
Hardly listen
Sigh. Wail.

Teach, dancing
Fly, dreaming

Stand. Sing.
Simmer. Stew.
Weed. Weep.
Sleep. Screw.

Isn't it good what a body can do

Isn't it good
What a body can do

Roy Webster Columbia River Cross Channel 09/07/2009
Lee Ann McNerney

Not a race, nor a contest, but just an achievement to accomplish a goal-and thus bring appeasement that lies dormant in everyone's soul. (Roy Webster, 1984)

I awoke at 3:00 a.m. in the morning the day of the Annual Columbia Channel Swim on Labor Day. I had faith that I could swim 1.1 miles from the shores of Washington to Hood River Oregon. Roy Webster, a Hood River Valley orchardist, was the founder of this swim. An avid swimmer certainly was not scared the first time he challenged his young buddies in 1942 to swim across the river for the pure enjoyment of exercise. He continued to swim across the river every year into his mid 80's. I was aware of this channel swim and subconsciously always wanted to participate in it.

Similar to Roy Webster's experience, on September 9th, at 5:45 a.m. it was my destiny to jump into the fourth largest river (by volume) in the world with almost 500 other swimmers from different parts of the world. That day I kept asking myself, "am I really going to do this? What if I don't succeed? Everyone would be so disappointed if I stopped and had to be rescued by a sailboat or kayak." I felt as nervous as the day I ran in the NAIA National Cross Country Race in 1982 with my teammates from Pacific Lutheran University in Madison, Wisconsin. Little did I know that I would have those same nervous feelings twenty seven years later. I had transitioned from running to swimming after losing my left leg in 1989 in a bus accident in the Dominican Republic as a Peace Corp volunteer. After recovering from that accident, I concentrated on swimming as my athletic outlet. In the years preceding the river swim I swam on master swim teams and many competitions around the world, including the Paraolympics, so training for a little over a mile was no big deal. However, like others, over the years, I had heard terrible stories about people drowning in the Columbia River. Of course there was a lane lined for the swimmers and boats all along the lane for safety.

A sternwheeler was made available for the swimmers to cross over from Oregon to the Washington Shore where I would begin my swim. I met many nice people who were as excited and anxious as I was. We gave each other encouragement and wished each other good luck that we would finish the swim. After meeting these new acquaintances it was my turn to begin. I hopped upon the railing of the sternwheeler with the other swimmers in my assigned group, dropped my crutches and knew at that moment there was no turning back. The starting whistle blew and I jumped into the great dark depths of the Columbia River. That was a shocking moment because I had not experienced jumping into a deep river. The water was murky, it was a deep dive, and totally different than anything I had done before. I couldn't get to the surface fast enough. I went into survival mode and kicked my leg as hard as I could while using my arms and hands to get to the surface of the dark water. "Let's go Lee Ann, let's do this thing," I said to myself." I swam at a moderate pace, and with each stroke I became more confident and faster. I was pleased that I was passing other swimmers even though this was probably one of the first times I was not racing against other swimmers. As I finished the swim I felt the same joy I had had in running past the finish line in 1982. I had achieved yet another challenge I had set out to accomplish in my lifetime. I am grateful to people like Roy Webster who preclude the mindset that people with disabilities cannot achieve their goals.

The Second Annual Irv Johnson Memorial Tubesetting Competition
Carol Lauritzen

The Second Annual Irv Johnson Memorial
Tubesetting Competition
was held on Sunday,
at the Bryan Johnson ditch
7 miles north of town
on old Highway 7.
The young adult division
required a rematch
because the friendly rivals
tied at 25 tubes in 1 minute, 4 seconds
with no dead ones.
In the children's division,
Darren set 10 tubes in 39 seconds.
"He'll hire out more expensive
next year."
Joey had all 10 running in 29 flat.
"Well, summer wages just went up."
But his little sister knew his worth,
"I bet he's all wore out now."
Only 3 entered the women's division.
"I've did it when I had to
but I'm not doing it now."

In red t-shirt, cut-off jeans
and irrigator boots.
Kathy joked "I have 3 tan lines,
the high boots, the low boots
and the tennis shoes."
25 tubes in 1:14 earned her
a $15.00 gift certificate.
The men's event came with hot air.
"I'd been faster except the wind
caught the bill of my cap."
"Right, Dennis, but you were going
downwind."
"It's bending over that big middle
that slows you down."
The honoree's son, "Kermit the Frog,"
makes "49 seconds flat
as the time to beat."
He claimed his mother's kiss and
the traveling trophy
for the second year.
The Co-op grilled burgers and beans
as the youngsters took a dunking
in the murky green ditch water
under the wide blue sky.

Conversation with Poets
and Other Marvelous Women
Kerri Jo Wenger

I'd so like
to invite
Diana Der-Hovanessian
to dinner

just for the pleasure
of saying her name
with that of the Mary Elinore Smith Poetry
Prize,
which she won for a poem
that celebrates words
and the voices of people
who breathe them being.

I'd ask her
like a cub reporter,
where she was born
("She was born bilingual but…")

and how
she bottles the yearnings
that turn into poems
inked with laser-precision
under the fingers
garnered, perhaps
from that place between
language
and learning
her Translation of meanings
overlapped by the musics
of spacing, and sound.

Newhall on a Sunday Afternoon
Michael Jaeger

The family unbelted
in the '56 yellow Ford wagon,
Smoking down the foothills,
On to Sepulveda, through old LA,
Destination: 12th street near Pico,
off Olympic.

Up the broad concrete porch steps,
Through the springy green screen door
Into the front room,
Between soft chairs, knicknacks and doilies,
Surrounded by the exotic dancers
on the wall,
There Grandma Louella stood,
Six foot, straight as a lamppost,
Long sateen dress and full apron,
Flaming red hair scared white
from a white-knuckle life
From her double Dublin grin,
"Hot tigedy, you finally got here."

She'd wrap me close and squeeze me
like toothpaste.
The smell of spices on her apron,
"Kiss me, I'm Irish!" Her signature phrase.
The bristle on her chin tingled on my cheek.

Grandma hustled up Sunday lunch--alone,
The lemon meringue
and savory chicken thigh
Recipes that had lured my father,
Were off limits to mom.

Grandpa Eddie shook my hand
Told his patented joke,
"Sit down and make yourself miserable."
He'd quaff his ale and ring up another quip.
With every glass
my parents' brows furrowed deeper.
We kids called him "Whimpy."
I never understood until decades later:
He was a Humberger, hence hamburger,
And Whimpy,
Popeye's hamburger eating pal.

"Dinner's on!"
Grandma's stories flew around the table,
Twenty-five years had passed,
        yet the details were still fresh to her:
When Ott got rammed in the butt
        by the one-eyed old sheep,
The time Dorothy pulled Harold from the
burning house,
When the moonshiners stashed the hooch
in the wash and the kids spied,

How Earhart's plane crash-landed
        and Ott fixed the propeller.
How Harold's sledgehammer
missed the chisel and hit Ott in the forehead.
The sheep herding, the trick pony riding,
        the sagebrush cutting,
Life in great depression Utah.
As the stories flowed, Louella glowed.
Dad growled, "Ah, Ma,"
We kids wide-eyed at the hundredth telling.

After food and story,
Lawrence Welk, Myron Florin,
Jackie Gleason—Crazy Guggenheim,
maybe Ed Sullivan and Topogigio.
Louella beamed, "That Myron Florin—
        he can sure play the accordion."
A heavenly smile, eyes in upward adoration,
she sang,
 "I see the Harbor Lights…"
"My boy Ray could sure sing."
We'd eat our pie and ice cream,
Grandma would open her See's chocolates,
And for kids, presents.

When the June Taylor dancers
with legs akimbo,
Ended their routine, it was time to go.
"Come here, you little fartheels,"
Grandma beckoned me
for a bookend squeeze.

A kiss goodbye and wave from the porch.
My sister and I negotiated
        the back seat geography
While parents wrestled over grandma's way.
The long ride home—Bob's Big Boy the
halfway mark.

23rd Street
Scott Smith

The Politician
Ray Brown

Flapping arms,
With little sagacity.
Puking invectives
Of nonsense, not rhyme.
He seeks the truth.

But, the truth,
Ever anxious,
Does not return the favor.
But instead, evades.

Consternation and platitudes
Are the hopes for the future
With incisive lack of wit
And challenge of mind.

This politician
Wags his tongue
Frog-like
Snaring the fly,
But missing the point

Friends in Miniature: Poetic Portraits
Karyn Gomez

Niles

Unintentionally elitist
Love eludes him, daunted by his genius
Lonely, he asks me,
"Am I intimidating?"
I lie

David

Roller coaster of emotional overload
A friend to grip my hand on the up hills
And scream with me on the down hills

Jess

Tough, athletic, popular, cool
Terrified me at the age of 13
Had to be her friend
 'cause I was scared not to be

Chris

Always good for a laugh
Biting sarcasm and caustic wit

It didn't hurt that he was gorgeous

Split Rock Café
Carol Lauritzen

The puddle covering the welcome mat at
the Split Rock Cafe might have been a
warning to other travelers. But the need for
coffee after two hours of viewing Wyoming
through car windows fogged by a cold, gray
mist had dampened my caution. Eight pairs
of eyes turn in the sudden silence. Only
three of the tables are occupied but the
chairs at other tables are turned at odd
angles to the room. I move toward the table
by the window, pull the chairs in to it and sit
down. From the table at the back, a figure
rises. Her apron proclaims waitress but the
grease line across the belly proclaims cook.
She moves behind the counter snagging
menus and water as she passes. "I'll have a
short stack." "They're big," she says, "one
will be a-plenty." I nod in agreement.

There's not going to be an argument from me.

The sound of conversation rises as though someone is gradually turning the volume knob. In the center of the room are two older Indians and a cowboy. One decides his desire to finish telling his story is stronger than his interest in strangers. "Yup--this new road up to the lake is just wide enough for a truck to pass between the rocks." The mud on his boots confirms his having to chain up. "Game and fish were surprised when they found me up there. They didn't chain up and got stuck. Yep...this new road ain't no place for them city guys." He's smug and snug in his Chute-out jacket--this rugged rider of bucking trucks.

The little table by the door is crowded. The brunette there asks if the three guys are from Lander. She knows she's seen them before but needs to put them in place. The dark-haired man at the table grins at her. He lifts his quart of Jack Daniels off the floor to sweeten his coffee. He offers it to the others and grins again, this time for the other occupant of the table. She's resting her auburn locks on her arm on the table. The peacock blue boots ought to be on other feet this morning.

Another figure rises from the back table, drifts behind the counter to the refrigerator, and pops a Pepsi. She's all denim-covered legs topped by a grimy baseball cap. "Hey, redheaded stepsister, want to play darts? Wait, before we start...do you know how to play?" "Pool," is the muttered reply. "Well, piss on you. I'll play by myself." The Grinner volunteers to play pool with Red. "Got any quarters?" "No." "That's okay. Hey, Marge, will you put a couple beers on my tab but give it to me in quarters."

Cowboy asks Brunette, "How do you get to Sweet Creek?" Before she can answer Legs slides back into the room. "Go down this road past 3 cattle guards and turn left" as she returns to darts.

Cowboy again, "Who owns it?" Brunette cocks her thumb. "Her dad. Me and Bill was up there while back and seen 250 head of wild horses. Pretty place."

My breakfast order arrives. It is a cake-- wide and tall, made light and metallic with an abundance of baking powder. No need for syrup. It's already flavored with small town, Wyoming.

Mothering Springs
Kerri Jo Wenger

Pocket Mama's our best nanny goat.
Call her Amaltheia: She,

shoulder dipping, gait askew,
steps and sways in dignity

shepherds perfect,
thrifty twins each season

mothers hers
as if they were
the gods themselves

suckles and
stands watch
with quiet purpose.

And
at journey's end
she is the kind
who gives her hide,
her life
to fortify and armor:

And so her children are heroic,
are the heralds of the best
that is to come.

Poem

Ralph Woodward

The sound of the wind moving
      through the grass
Flowers swaying ever so gently
Rocking the butterfly
      to the rhythm of the wind.

Crows agitated in a hillside thicket of trees
      as a hawk swoops from above
          chasing it away
order restored.

The gray, pitted rock covered in green and
brown lichen
  staring into the sky
      not caring why
        nor
          concerned with my existence.

Kauai #2
Heather Stanhope

Picking Huckleberries
Carol Lauritzen

The poem for a mountain morning
    of patient picking
Of small purple berries from the silences
    between the leaves
Of ground-hugging bushes ought
    to be obvious.

What it should say is that each berry
    is a moment saved,
A bit of peace dropped in the pail
To be carefully saved and served
    on a gray wintry day.

It should say that huckleberry picking is
    a meditation--
The soft plunk of each tiny berry
    tapping at the soul.
"You are no more in the universe than this."

It should say that the silent figure
    bending low
Is seeking the name of god
    in the huckleberries
Under the towering pines
    with hawks parting the sky.

Time

M. Ruth Davenport

In darkness, in the morning bookend
    of my day
I trundled papers, books,
    the stuff of teaching
To another day's endeavor
    in gratitude
The frost of autumn escapes my lips
I smile my thanks for another chance
I pass a small tree on the berm,
laden with the tiniest
    of shadowed leaves
No hint of breeze, no coaxing
    from an unseen whisper
In unison, unanimously,
    each leaf takes flight
In swirling, slow motion of presence,
    of lingering,
    of savoring the journey
To a new earth-bound home,
    they fall, they rest
There was no wind
It was simply time.

Contributors

Ray Brown
Outdoors
Loves to read
Determined
Family-oriented
Avid sports fan
Resolute
Traveler--loves Europe
 But, "brevity is the soul of wit,"
        thus, I close.

M. Ruth Davenport
   Ruthi loves to learn (the stack of books
never ends!) and she thrives when she can
help others with their learning. She is a
partner in an equine therapeutic center, runs
a designing business, and teaches music to
learners of all ages. She conducts research in
literacy learning and tutors students from
preschool through adults in reading and
writing.

Jan Dinsmore

When she was a little girl, Jan wanted to be either a movie star or a teacher. We are glad she chose the latter, although Kerri's young son thinks she looks like a movie star. Jan loves being warm, pushing learners to be great teachers, and delighting other people. Jan's little known accomplishments include making great ebelskivers and award-winning artwork - because her friends submit her pieces.

Karyn Gomez

The inauspicious beginning of her academic career as a kindergarten drop out did not curb Karyn Gomez's enthusiasm for school. Once she returned to school as a first grader, she never left again. Her school career is in its 42nd year, including 15 years in sixth grade. She has spent much of her career adopting strays, both four-legged and two-legged, at home and at school. She looks forward to many more years of sharing her passion for teaching and advocating for kids of all ages.

Michael Jaeger

A rock pick and shovel, a butterfly net, a pair of binoculars, a topo map, a mushroom knife; a table saw, lathe, nail gun, welder; an oscilloscope, soldering iron, signal tracer, meter--these are the tools Michael prefers over email, memos, and meetings.

Carol Lauritzen

When she isn't teaching online graduate literacy classes, Carol reads, writes, hikes, skis, gardens, hunts for mushrooms and wild berries, sings, and dances with a folklore group. She grew up setting tubes and riding the range in her grandfather's Olds 88 but fortunately she did not inherit a finicky stomach. Carol enjoys eating in unusual places around the world.

Lee Ann McNerney

In her spare time, Lee Ann enjoys taking Spanish classes. Depending on the season of her life she is either swimming or going to Weight Watchers! She daydreams about traveling.

Sharon Porter

Sharon can be found plucking away on her ukulele, reading young adult literature, trying out the newest technology, and singing and playing bass in several bands. In her spare time, she is mom to two Chiweenies and likes to wear out her luggage.

Scott Smith

Scott Smith joined the CUESTE (undergraduate teacher education) team on the BMCC campus in 2008. Along with education, photography has always been an interest. For over 20 years, in addition to teaching, Scott and his wife (also a teacher) operated a studio, photographing weddings across the Pacific Northwest. If not in a classroom, Scott and Sue are with a camera sailing on their boat not far away.

Heather Stanhope

Heather is the Advising Coordinator and Teacher Licensure Officer for EOU's College of Education. In her spare time she loves fitness (walking, biking, skiing, aerobics, swimming & diving), music (ukelele), photography and Facebook. She volunteers her time to several worthy community service activities. This year a special focus has been collaboration to solidify two local tour routes for the statewide Scenic Bikeways designation. After 12 years she still very much enjoys her job-- colleagues & clientele make it happen ...and it does help finance her passion for travel to new scuba diving locations!

Kerri Jo Wenger

Kerri seems to spend equal time teaching future teachers and chasing kids human and caprine on her family's eastern Oregon farm. She loves teaching and learning in rural schools and multicultural classrooms, and really solid fences.

Donald Wolff

Donald teaches a good deal online and students generally find little advantage in meeting him face-to-face. But often you can find him in La Grande walking his Golden Retriever, Sugar, or riding out to Ladd Marsh on his ten-speed, with the upright, old-man handlebars, not the curved racing ones--he's no longer built for speed.

Ralph Woodward

From the vantage point of recent retirement, Ralph can see a long and illustrious career as a teacher. He wrote this poem while on a field trip with students at Ladd Marsh. Ralph enjoys woodworking, walking in the woods and gardening.